D0532124

Pancakes
& Waffles

Pancakes & Waffles

Delicious ideas for breakfast, brunch and beyond

with recipes by
Hannah Miles

RYLAND PETERS & SMALL
LONDON • NEW YORK

Designer Paul Stradling
Production Controller David Hearn
Art Director Leslie Harrington
Editorial Director Julia Charles
Publisher Cindy Richards

Indexer Hilary Bird

Published in 2017 by
Ryland Peters & Small
20–21 Jockey's Fields
London WC1R 4BW
and
341 E 116th St
New York
NY 10029

www.rylandpeters.com

Recipe collection compiled by Julia Charles
Text © Hannah Miles, Amy Ruth Finegold, Laura Washburn
and Jenna Zoe 2014, 2017
Design and photographs © Ryland Peters & Small 2017

Note: recipes written by Hannah Miles and featured in this
book previously appeared in *Pancakes, Crêpes, Waffles &
French Toast*, published by Ryland Peters & Small in 2014

ISBN: 978-1-84975-822-2

10 9 8 7 6 5 4 3 2 1

Printed in China

A CIP record for this book is available from the British Library.
US Library of Congress CIP data has been applied for.

33614057817446

Notes

• Both British (Metric) and American (Imperial plus US cups) are
included in these recipes for your convenience, however it is very
important to work with one set of measurements and not alternate
between both within a recipe.

• All eggs are medium (UK) or large (US), unless otherwise
specified. Uncooked or partially cooked eggs should not be served to
the very old, frail, young children, pregnant women or those with
compromised immune systems.

• All spoon measurements are level unless otherwise specified.

• When a recipe calls for the grated zest of citrus fruit, buy unwaxed
fruit and wash well before using. If you can only find treated fruit,
scrub well in warm soapy water before using.

• Ovens should be preheated to the specified temperatures. We
recommend using an oven thermometer. If using a fan-assisted oven,
adjust temperatures according to the manufacturer's instructions.

Recipe & photography credits

All recipes and text by Hannah Miles, except page 11 Amy Ruth Finegold,
page 16 Laura Washburn and page 19 Jenna Zoe.

All photography by Steve Painter, except page 5 Jonathan Gregson, page 17
Kate Whitaker and pages 3, 10 and 18 Clare Winfield.

Contents

Introduction

For almost as long as I can remember I have loved making pancakes and waffles. Pancakes were one of the first things I learnt to cook and I used to make them when I came home from school, eating them hot from the pan and drenched in syrup. The best thing about them is that they are great quick-fix recipes, needing only a few simple ingredients from the storecupboard and fridge – flour, milk, eggs – as a base and then you can add flavour with whatever else you have to hand, whether it's cheese, bacon, butter or syrup. There are few more delicious home-cooked dishes to serve for a relaxed weekend breakfast, or to friends when hosting a brunch party. And pancakes and waffles are not just for the morning – their versatility means that with a few clever twists they also make delicious and satisfying lunch, teatime or supper dishes.

What are pancakes & waffles?

Pancakes are served all around the world and have appeared in recipe books for centuries. There are two types of pancake – crêpes, which are traditional French pancakes, made with a light batter spread out very thinly in a pan, and American pancakes (or griddle cakes), which are made with a denser batter that includes raising agents. The resulting pancakes are thick, light and fluffy. The recipes in this book are all American-style pancakes, as not only are they delicious with lashings of sauce poured over them, but they can also be filled, which opens up lots of exciting sweet and savoury flavour combination possibilities! Waffles are also made with a heavy batter, but lightened with whisked egg whites. You use a waffle iron to cook them and there are two main types to choose from – electric or stove-top. Both come in a variety of patterns: rectangular; circular; heart-shaped; or even waffle fingers. I find that electric waffle irons have better temperature control than stove-top waffle pans but the choice is yours. The beauty of waffle batter is that it can be flavoured with almost anything, transforming a simple batter into something very special.

Hints & tips

• The quantities of ingredients given in the recipes here are guidelines only, as the number of pancakes or waffles each batch of batter will make very much depends on the size of your pan or waffle iron. If you want to make only a few waffles or pancakes, simply halve the ingredients where necessary. If you want more, double it.

• Ensure that you leave the batter to rest for the specified time as this allows the gluten in the flour to relax and, if using baking powder, air bubbles to form in the batter.

• Take care not to over-grease your pan. I usually add butter or oil to the pan before I start and then carefully wipe it with a paper towels to remove any excess. You'll find that the first pancake or waffle cooked is never as good as the later ones and this is because there is less fat in the pan as you go along.

• Make sure that you don't turn pancakes over too quickly. The batter on the top of the pancake should be almost completely cooked before you flip.

• Always serve your pancakes and waffles immediately!

American pancakes with whipped maple butter

This classic American-style pancake is light and fluffy and served with lashings of real maple syrup. Here, they are also served with whipped maple butter. Whipped butters are a delicious treat and can be made in many flavours. You need to serve them straight away rather than storing them in the refrigerator though, otherwise the butter will set and lose its light texture.

160 g/1¼ cups self-raising/rising flour, sifted

1 teaspoon baking powder

1 egg, separated

1 teaspoon vanilla extract/vanilla bean paste

60 g/scant ⅓ cup caster/granulated sugar

a pinch of salt

250 ml/1 cup milk

3 tablespoons melted butter, plus extra for frying

for the maple butter

115 g/1 stick butter

60 ml/¼ cup maple syrup, plus extra to serve

60 g/½ cup icing/confectioners' sugar, sifted

a large frying pan/skillet or griddle

MAKES 12

To make the pancake batter, put the flour, baking powder, egg yolk, vanilla extract/vanilla bean paste, caster/granulated sugar, salt and milk in a large mixing bowl and whisk together. Add in the melted butter and whisk again. The batter should have a smooth, dropping consistency.

In a separate bowl, whisk the egg white to stiff peaks. Gently fold the whisked egg white into the batter mixture using a spatula. Cover and put in the refrigerator to rest for 30 minutes.

For the maple butter, whisk together the butter, maple syrup and icing/confectioners' sugar using an electric whisk until light and creamy. This is best made shortly before serving.

When you are ready to serve, remove your batter mixture from the refrigerator and stir once. Put a little butter in a large frying pan/skillet set over medium heat. Allow the butter to melt and coat the base of the pan, then ladle small amounts of the rested batter into the pan, leaving a little space between each, or if you want to make larger pancakes you can fill the pan to make one at a time. Cook until the underside of each pancake is golden brown and a few bubbles start to appear on the top – this will take about 2–3 minutes. Turn the pancakes over using a spatula and cook on the other side until golden brown. Cook the remaining batter in the same way in batches until it is all used up, adding a little butter to the pan each time, if required.

Serve the pancakes in a stack with a little maple butter and a drizzle of maple syrup on top.

Buckwheat & flaxseed pancakes

This wholesome recipe for pancakes ups the nutrition factor by taking out white wheat flour as the base and adding wholegrain flours and flaxseeds. Using almond milk makes them perfect for anyone excluding or limiting dairy in their diets and gives a pleasingly light and fluffy texture. Serve hot with fresh blueberries and don't skimp on the maple syrup – that's the best bit!

50 g/⅓ cup potato starch

½ teaspoon bicarbonate of soda/baking soda

1½ teaspoons baking powder

70 g/½ cup buckwheat flour

60 g/½ cup brown rice flour

3 tablespoons milled flaxseeds

½ teaspoon sea salt

1 teaspoon cinnamon

480 ml/2 cups almond milk

2 eggs (see Note)

1 teaspoon vanilla extract

vegetable oil, for shallow frying

maple syrup, to taste

a handful of blueberries, to serve (optional)

MAKES 12

Sift the potato starch, bicarbonate of soda/baking soda and baking powder into a mixing bowl. Add in the remaining dry ingredients and set aside. In another bowl, combine the almond milk, eggs and vanilla extract. Add the wet into the dry ingredients gradually and whisk to a thick batter.

Heat the oil in a frying pan/skillet over a medium–high heat. Drop the batter from a spoon into the pan to form round circles. Cook until small bubbles form on the top of each pancake. Flip and cook for a further 3 minutes or until golden brown in colour.

Serve immediately, stacked on a plate and drizzled with maple syrup. Blueberries make a tasty addition, if desired, and are a powerful antioxidant.

Note: If you prefer not to use eggs you could use egg replacer or make a flax-egg mix by combining 2 tablespoons of ground flaxseed with 6 tablespoons of water.

Oatmeal pancakes with berry compote

These are great breakfast pancakes – with oatmeal soaked in milk mixed into the batter and toasted candied oats on top. Served with a warm berry compote and crème fraîche or yogurt, they are the perfect pancakes to make in the summer, when you have a glut of fresh soft red berries to use up.

370–400 ml/1½ cups milk

200 g/1½ cups self-raising/rising flour, sifted

2 teaspoon baking powder

1 egg

a pinch of salt

1 tablespoon caster/granulated sugar

3 tablespoons melted butter, plus extra for frying

crème fraîche or plain yogurt, to serve (optional)

for the compote

500 g/4 cups summer berries (raspberries, blueberries, strawberries and blackberries in any combination of your choosing), stalks removed

250 ml/1 cup water

100 g/½ cup caster/granulated sugar

1 teaspoon vanilla extract/vanilla bean paste

freshly squeezed juice of 1 lemon

for the toasted oats

60 g/½ cup oatmeal

50 g/¼ tablespoon caster/granulated sugar

a large frying pan/skillet or griddle

MAKES 10

Begin by preparing the compote. Put the summer berries in a saucepan or pot set over a medium heat with the water, sugar, vanilla extract/vanilla bean paste and lemon juice. Simmer until the sugar has dissolved and the fruit is just starting to soften but still holds its shape. This will take about 5 minutes. Set aside to cool then store in the refrigerator until you are ready to serve.

For the toasted oats, place the oats and sugar in a dry frying pan/ skillet set over a medium heat and toast for a few minutes until the sugar starts to caramelize the oats. Remove from the heat and set aside to cool.

Soak half of the toasted oats in 250 ml/1 cup of the milk for about 30 minutes, until plump. Reserving the rest of the oats for the pancake batter.

To make the pancake batter, put the flour, baking powder, egg, salt, caster/ granulated sugar and milk-soaked oats in a large mixing bowl and whisk together. Add in the melted butter and whisk again. Gradually add the remaining milk until you have a smooth, pourable batter. Be careful not to make the batter too thin when adding the remaining milk – you may not need it all. Cover and put in the refrigerator to rest for 30 minutes.

When you are ready to serve, remove your batter mixture from the refrigerator and stir once. Put a little butter in a large frying pan/skillet set over a medium heat. Allow the butter to melt and coat the base of the pan, then ladle small amounts of the batter into the pan. Sprinkle some of the reserved toasted oats over the top of the pancake and cook until the underside is golden brown and a few bubbles start to appear on the top – this will take about 2–3 minutes. Turn the pancake over using a spatula and cook on the other side until golden brown. Keep the pancakes warm while you cook the remaining batter in the same way, adding a little more butter to the pan each time if required.

Serve the pancakes with the cooled berry compote and crème fraîche or yogurt, as preferred.

Granola pancakes with salty honey sauce

These are one of my favourite breakfast pancakes. They have a crunchy, oaty top and are served with a delicious, buttery, honey sauce. You can also add raisins, sultanas, dried berries and cherries to the batter for an extra fruity tang.

160 g/1¼ cups self-raising/rising flour, sifted

1 teaspoon baking powder

1 egg, separated

1 tablespoon orange blossom honey

a pinch of salt

250 ml/1 cup milk

3 tablespoons melted butter, plus extra for frying

120–150 g/1½ cups granola

for the sauce

60 g/4 tablespoons butter

3½ tablespoons clear honey

½ teaspoon salt

120 ml/½ cup double/heavy cream

a large frying pan/skillet or griddle

MAKES 6

To make the pancake batter, put the flour, baking powder, egg yolk, honey, salt and milk in a large mixing bowl and whisk together. Add in the melted butter and whisk again. The batter should have a smooth, dropping consistency.

In a separate bowl, whisk the egg white to stiff peaks. Gently fold the whisked egg white into the batter mixture using a spatula. Cover and put in the refrigerator to rest for 30 minutes.

For the sauce, heat the butter and honey in a small saucepan or pot until the butter has melted. Then add the salt and whisk in the cream over the heat. Keep the pan on the heat but turn it down to low to keep the sauce warm until you are ready to serve.

When you are ready to serve, remove your batter mixture from the refrigerator and stir once. Put a little butter in a large frying pan/skillet set over a medium heat. Allow the butter to melt and coat the base of the pan, then ladle the batter into the pan and sprinkle a little granola on top of the pancake. Cook until the underside of the pancake is golden brown and a few bubbles start to appear on the top – this will take about 2–3 minutes. Turn the pancake over using a spatula and cook on the other side until golden brown. Keep the pancake warm while you cook the remaining batter, adding a little more butter to the pan each time if necessary.

Serve the pancakes with the warm honey sauce poured over the top.

Multigrain pancakes

Get off to a healthy start in the morning with these easy and nutritious pancakes. They are delicious served simply with a little melted butter and a drizzle of maple syrup, but you can also vary this basic recipe by adding fresh berries, banana, nuts or dried fruit to the batter just before cooking.

120 g/¾ cup wholemeal/whole-wheat flour

65 g/½ cup oatbran

85 g/1½ cups plain/all-purpose flour

45 g/¼ cup cornmeal

1 teaspoon baking powder

½ teaspoon bicarbonate of soda/baking soda

a pinch of fine sea salt

400 ml/1¾ cups milk

2 eggs

2 tablespoons vegetable oil

MAKES 15

Put all of the dry ingredients in a mixing bowl. Whisk together the milk, eggs and oil in a separate bowl or jug/pitcher.

Pour the milk mixture onto the flour mixture and beat until blended but still a little lumpy.

Heat a large non-stick frying pan/skillet and wipe or brush lightly with vegetable oil. Add a ladleful of the pancake batter. Cook until bubbles just appear on the surface then turn over and cook for 1–2 minutes on the other side. Repeat until all of the batter has been used.

Serve immediately with butter and maple syrup, fruit coulis or jam.

Free-from protein pancakes

Now everyone can enjoy breakfast pancakes! This recipe is gluten-free, dairy-free and free from refined sugar. Given a nutritional boost with the addition of protein powder, these make the ideal start to the day for runners and gym bunnies everywhere! Serve with your choice of fresh fruit or chocolate chips for an indulgent yet healthy treat.

6 tablespoons gluten-free plain/all-purpose flour of choice

1 scoop of protein powder of choice

½ tablespoon xylitol or stevia, or other granulated sweetener

½ teaspoon baking powder

a pinch of salt

1 small banana

1 tablespoon non-dairy milk of choice

1 teaspoon vanilla extract

½ teaspoon coconut oil

berries of choice and maple syrup, or dark/bittersweet chocolate chips, to serve

MAKES 3–4

In a bowl, combine the flour, protein powder, sweetener, baking powder and salt.

Separately, mash the banana until no lumps remain, then add the milk and vanilla extract.

Mix the wet ingredients into the bowl of dry ingredients until well combined.

Melt the coconut oil in a frying pan over medium heat so that it coats the bottom of the pan. Spoon a quarter of the pancake batter at a time into the pan, then flip the pancake over when you see it start to bubble. Cook until golden underneath. Remove the pancake from the pan and keep it warm while you make the remaining pancakes with the rest of the batter.

Serve with berries and a touch of maple syrup for a healthy option, or dark/bittersweet chocolate chips for a treat.

Buttermilk pancakes with salmon & horseradish cream

Little pancakes topped with smoked salmon make fantastic canapés. For a more indulgent version why not serve large, fluffy buttermilk pancakes seasoned with chives and topped with thick slices of smoked salmon and horseradish cream? This is great as a brunch dish or a light lunch or supper.

170 g/1⅓ cups self-raising/rising flour, sifted

1 teaspoon baking powder

2 eggs, separated

200 ml/⅔ cup buttermilk

2 teaspoon caster/granulated sugar

1 tablespoon finely chopped chives, plus extra for sprinkling

100 ml/⅓ cup milk

250 ml/1 cup crème fraîche or sour cream

1 heaped tablespoon creamed horseradish

1–2 tablespoons butter, for frying

400 g/2½ cups smoked salmon, to serve

1 lemon, sliced into wedges

sea salt and freshly ground black pepper, to taste

a large frying pan/skillet or griddle

SERVES 4

To make the pancake batter, put the flour, baking powder, egg yolks, buttermilk, caster/granulated sugar and chives in a large mixing bowl and whisk together. Season well with salt and pepper, then gradually add the milk until the batter is smooth and pourable.

In a separate bowl, whisk the egg whites to stiff peaks. Gently fold the whisked egg whites into the batter mixture using a spatula. Cover and put in the refrigerator to rest for 30 minutes.

For the horseradish cream, whisk together the crème fraîche and horseradish in a mixing bowl and season with salt and pepper.

When you are ready to serve, remove the batter mixture from the refrigerator and stir once. Put a little butter in a large frying pan/skillet set over a medium heat. Allow the butter to melt and coat the base of the pan, then ladle small amounts of the rested batter into the pan, leaving a little space between each. Cook until the underside of each pancake is golden brown and a few bubbles start to appear on the top – this will take about 2–3 minutes. Turn the pancake over using a spatula and cook on the other side until golden brown.

Serve the pancakes warm, topped with a generous spoon of the horseradish cream, slices of smoked salmon and wedge of lemon to squeeze over the top. Sprinkle with extra chopped chives and enjoy.

Beer & bacon pancakes

These pancakes really are very manly! In place of milk, beer is used to bind the batter. It gives the pancakes a savoury, malty flavour, and with the addition of salty bacon and sweet maple syrup, they really are the perfect sweet and savoury combination.

200 g/1½ cups smoked bacon lardons/diced pancetta

12 slices of smoked streaky bacon/bacon strips, to serve

160 g/1⅓ cups self-raising/rising flour, sifted

1 teaspoon baking powder

1 egg, separated

60 g/⅓ cup dark brown sugar

a pinch of salt

250 ml/1 cup beer

3 tablespoons melted butter, plus extra for frying

maple syrup, to drizzle

2 large frying pans/skillets or griddle

SERVES 6

Begin by frying all of the bacon in a dry frying pan/skillet – it will release sufficient oil as you cook it to prevent it sticking so you do not need to add any extra fat to the pan. Remove from the pan and put on a paper towel to remove any excess fat. Set aside while you prepare the batter.

To make the pancake batter, put the flour, baking powder, egg yolk, dark brown sugar, salt and beer in a large mixing bowl and whisk together. Add in the melted butter and cooked bacon lardons and whisk again. The batter should have a smooth, dropping consistency.

In a separate bowl, whisk the egg white to stiff peaks. Gently fold the whisked egg white into the batter mixture using a spatula. Cover and put in the refrigerator to rest for 30 minutes.

When you are ready to serve, remove your batter mixture from the refrigerator and stir gently. Put a little butter in a large frying pan/skillet set over a medium heat. Allow the butter to melt and coat the base of the pan, then ladle small amounts of the rested batter into the pan, leaving a little space between each. Cook until the underside of each pancake is golden brown and a few bubbles start to appear on the top – this will take about 2–3 minutes. Turn the pancake over using a spatula and cook on the other side until golden brown.

Serve the pancakes with streaky bacon/bacon strips and plenty of maple syrup.

Squash & goat's cheese pancakes

Perfect for lunch, these pancakes are topped with sour cream or crème fraîche and drizzled with delicious pumpkin seed oil. Use a mild, creamy goat's cheese so that the flavour is not overpowering. I love to use Halen Môn sea salt (available online) in this recipe as it is fragranced with cumin, nutmeg, paprika, cloves and cinnamon and goes really well with the spiced squash.

1 butternut squash, peeled and seeds removed (670 g/2½ lb), diced

2 tablespoons olive oil

1 teaspoon black onion seeds

a pinch of spiced sea salt or regular sea salt

4–5 curry leaves, crushed

1–2 garlic cloves, skins on

200 g/1⅔ cups self-raising/rising flour, sifted

2 teaspoons baking powder

1 egg

300 ml/1¼ cups milk

3 tablespoons melted butter, plus extra for greasing

125 g/1 cup soft goat's cheese

sour cream, to serve

a bunch of Greek basil leaves, to garnish

pumpkin seed oil, to drizzle

sea salt and freshly ground black pepper, to taste

an ovenproof roasting pan, greased

a large frying pan/skillet or griddle

SERVES 4

Preheat the oven to 180°C (350°F) Gas 4.

Put the diced butternut squash in the prepared roasting pan. Drizzle with the olive oil and sprinkle over the onion seeds, salt and curry leaves. Stir so that the squash is well coated in the oil and spices, then add the garlic cloves to the pan. Roast in the preheated oven for 35–45 minutes until the squash is soft and starts to caramelize at the edges. Leave to cool completely.

To make the pancake batter, put the flour, baking powder, egg and milk in a large mixing bowl and whisk together. Season with salt and pepper. Add the melted butter and whisk again. The batter should have a smooth, dropping consistency. Add about two thirds of the butternut squash to the batter and set aside.

Remove the skins from the garlic cloves and mash to a paste using a fork. Whisk into the batter then crumble in the goat's cheese. Mix together gently. Cover and put in the refrigerator to rest for 30 minutes.

Put a little butter in a large frying pan/skillet set over a medium heat. Allow the butter to melt and coat the base of the pan, then ladle spoonfuls of the rested batter into the pan, leaving a little space between each. Cook until the underside of each pancake is golden brown and a few bubbles start to appear on the top – this will take about 2–3 minutes. Turn the pancake over using a spatula and cook on the other side until golden brown.

Serve the pancakes, topped with a spoonful of sour cream, a few sprigs of basil and the reserved butternut squash. Drizzle with pumpkin seed oil and sprinkle with freshly ground black pepper.

Potato waffles with barbecue beans

Barbecue beans are among my top comfort foods. They are great as a side and remind me of nights spent open-air camping, with sausages and beans simmering over glowing embers. Served here with delicious potato waffles, this recipe is comfort food heaven.

2 baking potatoes

260 g/2 cups self-raising/rising flour, sifted

1 teaspoon baking powder

a pinch of salt

3 eggs, separated

300 ml/1¼ cups milk

60 g/4 tablespoons butter, melted

a handful of grated cheddar or Emmental cheese, to serve

for the beans

1 tablespoon olive oil

1 medium onion, peeled and finely sliced

1–2 garlic cloves, peeled and finely sliced

400 g/2 cups canned chopped tomatoes

2 tablespoons Worcestershire sauce

2 tablespoons soy sauce

40 g/¼ cup dark brown sugar

480 g/3¾ cups cooked cannellini beans, drained and rinsed

sea salt and freshly ground black pepper, to taste

an electric or stove-top waffle iron

a baking sheet lined with baking parchment

SERVES 4

Preheat the oven to 200°C (400°F) Gas 6.

Prick the potatoes with a fork and bake them in the preheated oven on the prepared baking sheet for 1 hour–1¼ hours (or in a microwave on full power for about 8 minutes per potato). Leave the potatoes to cool, then cut them open and remove the potato from the skins. Mash the flesh with a fork and discard the skins.

For the beans, heat the olive oil in a large saucepan or pot set over a medium heat. Add the sliced onion and cook until they turn translucent. Add the garlic to the pan and cook for a few minutes longer until the onion and garlic are lightly golden brown. Add the tomatoes to the pan and season well with salt and pepper. Add the Worcestershire sauce, soy sauce and dark brown sugar and simmer until the sauce becomes thick and syrupy. Put the beans in the sauce and simmer for a further 20 minutes. Keep the pan on the heat but turn it down to low to keep the beans warm until you are ready to serve.

In a large mixing bowl, whisk together the cooled mashed potato, flour, baking powder, salt, egg yolks, milk and melted butter until you have a smooth batter. In a separate bowl, whisk the egg white to stiff peaks. Gently fold the whisked egg whites into the batter mixture using a spatula.

Preheat the waffle iron and grease with a little butter.

Ladle some of the batter into the preheated waffle iron and cook for 3–5 minutes until golden brown. Keep the waffles warm while you cook the remaining batter.

Serve the waffles topped with the hot barbecue beans and grated cheese.

Ginger & sesame waffles with steak & dipping sauce

Steak and dipping sauce is a classic. These steaks are served with delicious sesame and ginger waffles to help mop up the juices.

3-cm/2-in piece of ginger, peeled

260 g/2 cups self-raising/rising flour, sifted

1 teaspoon baking powder

a pinch of salt

3 eggs, separated

375 ml/1½ cups milk

75 g/5 tablespoons butter, melted, plus extra for greasing

2 tablespoons finely chopped fresh coriander/cilantro

1 tablespoon sesame seeds

2–4 beef fillet steaks

sea salt and freshly ground black pepper, to taste

a bunch of fresh coriander/cilantro, to garnish

for the sauce

80 ml/scant ⅓ cup tamari soy sauce

60 ml/¼ cup Worcestershire sauce

60 ml/¼ cup maple syrup

1 heaped tablespoon tomato ketchup

1 tablespoon olive oil

1 tablespoon sesame seeds

1 tablespoon freshly chopped coriander/cilantro

freshly ground black pepper, to taste

an electric or stove-top waffle iron

a large frying pan/skillet or griddle

SERVES 4

To make the waffle batter, purée the ginger in a food processor, adding a little water if necessary. In a large mixing bowl, whisk together the flour, baking powder, salt, egg yolks, milk and melted butter until you have a smooth batter. Add the ginger purée, coriander/cilantro and sesame seeds and whisk again.

In a separate bowl, whisk the egg whites to stiff peaks. Gently fold the whisked egg whites into the batter mixture using a spatula.

Preheat the waffle iron and grease with a little butter.

Ladle some of the batter into the preheated waffle iron and cook for 2–3 minutes until golden brown. Keep the waffles warm while you cook the remaining batter and are ready to serve.

For the dipping sauce, put all of the ingredients in a bowl and whisk together.

Season the steaks with salt and pepper and sear in a frying pan/skillet set over a high heat. The cooking time will depend on how rare you like your meat. Sear for about 1–2 minutes on each side for rare and 3–4 minutes each side for well done, depending on the thickness of your steaks.

Slice the steaks very thinly and serve on top of 2 waffles per person with fresh coriander/cilantro and the dipping sauce on the side.

Huevos rancheros waffles

Huevos Rancheros or 'ranch eggs' are a traditional Mexican breakfast of spicy tomatoes with eggs served on corn tortillas. This recipe uses corn waffles in place of the tortillas. Although traditionally the tomatoes are served cooked, I prefer a tomato and avocado salsa as the taste is much fresher. Spice things up with a kick of piquant hot paprika!

160 g/1⅓ cups self-raising/rising flour, sifted

100 g/1 cup fine yellow cornflour/cornstarch

1 teaspoon bicarbonate of soda/baking soda

1 tablespoon caster/granulated sugar

3 eggs, separated

375 ml/1½ cups milk

60 g/5 tablespoons butter, melted

1 tablespoon olive or vegetable oil

8 eggs

70 g/scant 1 cup cheddar cheese, grated

sour cream, to serve

sea salt and freshly ground black pepper, to taste

for the salsa

4 large tomatoes, halved

2 ripe avocados

freshly squeezed juice of 2 limes

2 heaped tablespoons finely chopped fresh coriander/cilantro

½ teaspoon hot paprika, plus extra for sprinkling

an electric or stove-top waffle iron

a large frying pan/skillet or griddle

SERVES 4

To make the waffle batter, put the flour, cornflour, bicarbonate of soda, caster/granulated sugar, egg yolks, milk and melted butter in a large mixing bowl. Whisk until you have a smooth batter. Season with salt and pepper. In a separate mixing bowl, whisk the egg whites to stiff peaks and then gently fold into the batter a third at a time.

Preheat the waffle iron and grease with a little butter.

Ladle some of the batter into the preheated waffle iron and cook for 2–3 minutes until golden brown. Keep the waffles warm while you cook the remaining batter and are ready to serve.

For the salsa, remove the seeds from the halved tomatoes using a teaspoon and discard. Cut the hollowed out tomatoes into small pieces using a sharp knife. Prepare the avocado by removing the stones and skins and cutting the flesh into small pieces. Immediately mix the avocado with the lime juice and tomatoes so that it does not discolour. Add the coriander/cilantro, sprinkle over the paprika and stir in. Season with salt and pepper and set aside in the refrigerator until needed.

Heat the oil in a frying pan/skillet and fry the 4 eggs for 2–3 minutes until the whites of the eggs are cooked but the yolks are still soft and runny.

Place the waffles on plates and top with a generous portion of the salsa. Place the fried eggs on top and sprinkle over the grated cheese. Top with a spoonful of sour cream and a pinch of paprika, and serve straight away.

Welsh rarebit waffles

Welsh rarebit is so simple to prepare and makes a lovely supper, whether topping toast, a crumpet or, as in this recipe, a savoury waffle. Melted cheese with mustard and tangy Worcestershire sauce served with roasted vine tomatoes and a crisp green salad – what could be better?

200 g/1⅔ cups self-raising/rising flour, sifted

3 eggs, separated

250 ml/1 cup milk

70 g/5 tablespoons butter, melted

sea salt and freshly ground black pepper, to taste

for the roasted tomatoes

300 g/1⅔ cups vine cherry tomatoes

1–2 tablespoons olive oil

1 tablespoon balsamic glaze

1 tablespoon caster/granulated sugar

for the topping

300 g/3½ cups cheddar cheese, grated

1 egg

2 teaspoons wholegrain mustard

1 tablespoon Worcestershire sauce, plus extra to splash

an electric or stove-top waffle iron

SERVES 6

Begin by preparing the tomatoes. Preheat the oven to 180°C (350°F) Gas 4. Put the tomatoes in the roasting pan and drizzle with olive oil, the balsamic glaze and caster/granulated sugar. Season with salt and pepper and roast in the preheated oven for 20–30 minutes until the tomatoes are soft and their juices start to run. Keep warm until you are ready to serve.

To make the waffle batter, put the flour, egg yolks, milk and melted butter into a large mixing bowl. Whisk until you have a smooth batter. Season with salt and pepper. In a separate mixing bowl, whisk the egg whites to stiff peaks and then gently fold into the batter a third at a time.

Preheat the waffle iron and grease with a little butter.

Ladle some of the batter into the preheated waffle iron and cook for 2–3 minutes until golden brown. Keep warm while you cook the remaining batter and are ready to serve.

For the topping, put all the ingredients into a bowl and mix.

Spread a large spoonful of the cheese mixture over each waffle and place under a hot grill/broiler for a few minutes until the cheese melts and starts to turn golden brown. Watch carefully to make sure that the rarebit topping and waffle do not burn, turning the grill/broiler heat down if required. Splash the tops of the waffles with a few drops of Worcestershire sauce and serve immediately with the roasted tomatoes on the side.

Fresh & fruity

Buttermilk blueberry pancakes with blueberry lime sauce

Blueberries have a wonderful, explosive taste when fresh and in season, although they are available year-round in supermarkets and online. I have added a little lime juice to the sauce to give these pancakes extra zing, although you can omit this if you are lucky enough to have a good source of fresh, flavourful blueberries.

160 g/1¼ cups self-raising/rising flour, sifted

1 teaspoon baking powder

1 egg, separated

60 g/scant ⅓ cup caster/granulated sugar

a pinch of salt

200 ml/¾ cup milk

80 ml/5 tablespoons buttermilk

3 tablespoons melted butter, plus extra for frying

100 g/¾ cup fresh blueberries

for the sauce

300 g/2¼ cups blueberries

freshly squeezed juice of 3 limes

100 g/½ cup caster/granulated sugar

90 ml/6 tablespoons water

300 ml/1¼ cups double/heavy cream, whipped to soft peaks, to serve

a large frying pan/skillet or griddle

MAKES 12

Begin by making the sauce. Place the blueberries, lime juice and caster/granulated sugar in a saucepan or pot with the water and simmer over a gentle heat for about 5–10 minutes until the fruit is soft and the sauce is thick and syrupy.

To make the pancake batter, put the flour, baking powder, egg yolk, caster/granulated sugar, salt, milk and buttermilk in a large mixing bowl and whisk together. Add in the melted butter and whisk again. The batter should have a smooth, dropping consistency.

In a separate bowl, whisk the egg white to stiff peaks. Gently fold the whisked egg white into the batter mixture using a spatula. Cover and put in the refrigerator to rest for 30 minutes.

When you are ready to serve, remove your batter mixture from the refrigerator and stir once. Put a little butter in a large frying pan/skillet set over a medium heat. Allow the butter to melt and coat the base of the pan, then ladle small amounts of the batter into the pan, leaving a little space between each. Sprinkle a few blueberries over the top of the pancake and cook until the underside of each pancake is golden brown and a few bubbles start to appear on the top – this will take about 2–3 minutes. Turn the pancakes over using a spatula and cook on the other side until golden brown. Keep the pancakes warm while you cook the remaining batter in the same way, adding a little more butter to the pan each time, if required, and sprinkling each pancake with blueberries.

Serve the pancakes in a stack, drizzled with the blueberry sauce and a dollop of whipped cream.

Blackberry cream cheese pancakes

These pancakes have a hidden pocket of blackberry and cream cheese filling, a yummy surprise when you cut into them! Served with a tangy blackberry sauce and whipped cream, they are an indulgent pancake dessert.

160 g/1¼ cups self-raising/rising flour, sifted

1 teaspoon baking powder

1 egg, separated

2 tablespoons caster/granulated sugar

a pinch of salt

250 ml/1 cup milk

3 tablespoons melted butter, plus extra for frying

for the sauce & filling

300 g/2¼ cups blackberries

120 ml/½ cup water

100 g/½ cup caster/granulated sugar

100 g/½ cup cream cheese

250 ml/1 cup double/heavy cream, whipped to stiff peaks, to serve

a large frying pan/skillet or griddle

MAKES 6

Begin by making the blackberry sauce and filling. Place the blackberries in a saucepan or pot with the water and sugar together over a medium heat, and simmer for about 5 minutes until the fruit is soft and the liquid is syrupy. Leave to cool.

In a separate bowl, whisk together the cream cheese and 2 tablespoons of the cooled blackberries (fruit and syrup) to make the filling.

To make the pancake batter, put the flour, baking powder, egg yolk, caster/granulated sugar, salt and milk in a large mixing bowl and whisk together. Add in the melted butter and whisk again. The batter should have a smooth, dropping consistency.

In a separate bowl, whisk the egg white to stiff peaks. Gently fold the whisked egg white into the batter mixture using a spatula. Cover and put in the refrigerator to rest for 30 minutes.

When you are ready to serve, remove your batter mixture from the refrigerator and stir once. Put a little butter in a large frying pan/skillet set over a medium heat. Allow the butter to melt and coat the base of the pan, then ladle the batter into the pan and tip to spread the batter out into a circle. Place a spoonful of the blackberry filling in the centre of the pancake and carefully spread it out, leaving a gap between the filling and the edge of the pancake. Cover the filling with a little more pancake batter so that it is completely hidden. Cook until the underside of the pancake is golden brown and a few bubbles start to appear on the top – this will take about 2–3 minutes. Then turn the pancakes over using a spatula and cook on the other side until golden brown. Keep the pancakes warm while you cook the remaining batter in the same way, adding a little butter to the pan each time, if required.

Serve the pancakes with the reserved blackberry sauce and whipped cream on the side.

Lemon waffles

I like to top these lemony waffles with my homemade lemon curd. If preferred you can enjoy them with fresh blueberries and Greek-style yogurt as a less sweet breakfast option.

260 g/2 cups self-raising/rising flour, sifted

1 teaspoon baking powder

60 g/scant ⅓ cup caster/granulated sugar

a pinch of salt

3 eggs, separated

375 ml/1½ cups milk

75 g/5 tablespoons butter, melted

crème fraîche, to serve

icing/confectioners' sugar, for dusting

for the lemon curd (optional)

freshly squeezed juice and grated zest of 2 unwaxed lemons, the zest of 1 lemon reserved for the waffle batter

freshly squeezed juice and grated zest of 1 unwaxed lime

60 g/4 tablespoons butter

120 g/heaped ½ cup caster/granulated sugar

2 eggs

an electric or stove-top waffle iron

MAKES 8

Begin by making the lemon curd. Put the zest of 1 lemon in a heatproof bowl set over a saucepan or pot of simmering water. Add the lemon and lime juice, the butter and caster/granulated sugar. Simmer until the butter has melted and the sugar has dissolved and remove from the heat. In a separate mixing bowl, beat the eggs and stir 1 tablespoon at a time into the lemon butter mixture, whisking after each addition. Return the mixture to the heat and stir for a further 10–15 minutes until the curd is thick. Set aside to cool until you are ready to serve, then store in a sterilized jar in the refrigerator for up to 1 month.

To make the waffle batter, put the flour, reserved lemon zest, baking powder, caster/granulated sugar, salt, egg yolks, milk and melted butter in a large mixing bowl. Whisk until you have a smooth batter. In a separate mixing bowl, whisk the egg whites to stiff peaks and then gently fold into the batter a third at a time.

Preheat the waffle iron and grease with a little butter.

Ladle a small amount of the batter into the preheated waffle iron and cook the waffles for 2–3 minutes until golden brown. Keep the waffles warm while you cook the remaining batter in the same way.

Serve the waffles immediately with the lemon curd and a dollop of crème fraîche. Dust with icing/confectioners' sugar and enjoy! Alternatively, top with fresh blueberries and a generous scoop of thick and creamy Greek-style yogurt.

Orange waffles with roasted plums

Roasted plums made by my lovely Grandma was something I often ate for dessert when I was young. Such a simple dessert, but deliciously tangy, they are served here with orange and vanilla waffles and lashings of clotted cream.

260 g/2 cups self-raising/rising flour, sifted

1 teaspoon orange zest

3 eggs, separated

375 ml/1½ cups milk

1 teaspoon vanilla extract/vanilla bean paste

2 tablespoons caster/granulated sugar

a pinch of salt

60 g/4 tablespoons butter, melted

clotted cream, to serve

icing/confectioners' sugar, to dust

for the roasted plums

8 plums, halved and stones/pits removed

75 g/⅓ cup caster/granulated sugar

2 tablespoons water

freshly squeezed juice of 2 oranges

an ovenproof dish, greased

an electric or stove-top waffle iron

MAKES 8

Begin by preparing the plums. Preheat the oven to 180°C (350°F) Gas 4. Put the plum halves, cut side down, in the prepared roasting dish and sprinkle over 2 tablespoons sugar, the water and the orange juice. Bake in the preheated oven for 20 minutes until the fruit is soft but still holds its shape. Remove the plums from the dish and pour the cooking liquid into a saucepan or pot set over a medium heat. Simmer with 50 g/¼ cup of the caster/granulated sugar and 60 ml/¼ cup more water until you have a thin syrup. Set aside together with removed halved plums until you are ready to serve.

To make the waffle batter, put the flour, orange zest, egg yolks, milk, vanilla extract/vanilla bean paste, caster/granulated sugar, salt and melted butter into a large mixing bowl. Whisk until you have a smooth batter. In a separate mixing bowl, whisk the egg whites to stiff peaks and then gently fold into the batter a third at a time.

Preheat the waffle iron and grease with a little butter.

Ladle a small amount of the batter into the preheated waffle iron and cook the waffles for 2–3 minutes until golden brown. Keep the waffles warm while you cook the remaining batter in the same way.

Dust the waffles with icing/confectioners' sugar and serve immediately with the roasted plums, plum syrup and clotted cream.

Apricot & white chocolate waffles

Apricot and white chocolate go perfectly together. These waffles are bursting with apricot pieces and white chocolate chips, and are served with roasted apricots and an apricot butter. A complete apricot overload!

260 g/2 cups self-raising/rising flour, sifted

60 g/scant ⅓ cup caster/granulated sugar

a pinch of salt

3 eggs, separated

375 ml/1½ cups milk

1 tablespoon apricot jam/jelly

60 g/4 tablespoons butter, melted

100 g/⅔ cup white chocolate chips

80 g/½ cup dried apricots, finely chopped

icing/confectioners' sugar, to dust

for the roasted apricots & apricot butter

600 g/4 cups fresh apricots, halved and stones/pits removed

50 g/¼ cup caster/granulated sugar

50 g/3½ tablespoons butter

an electric or stove-top waffle iron

an ovenproof roasting dish, greased

MAKES 8

Begin by preparing the apricots. Preheat the oven to 180°C (350°F) Gas 4. Cut the apricots in half and remove the stones/pits. Place the apricot halves, cut side down, in the prepared roasting dish and sprinkle over the sugar. Cut the butter into small pieces and dot over the apricots. Bake in the preheated oven for about 25–30 minutes until the fruit is soft but still holds its shape. Remove from the oven then purée half of the apricots and the juices from the dish in a food processor until smooth to form the apricot butter. Set aside together with remaining halved apricots until you are ready to serve.

To make the waffle batter, put the flour, caster/granulated sugar, salt, egg yolks, milk, apricot jam/jelly and melted butter in a large mixing bowl. Whisk until you have a smooth batter. In a separate mixing bowl, whisk the egg whites to stiff peaks and then gently fold into the batter a third at a time. Fold in the white chocolate chips and dried apricot pieces.

Preheat the waffle iron and grease with a little butter.

Ladle a small amount of the batter into the preheated waffle iron and cook the waffles for 3–5 minutes until golden brown. Keep the waffles warm while you cook the remaining batter in the same way, stirring the batter each time to mix in the apricot pieces and chocolate chips.

Serve the waffles immediately, dusted with icing/confectioners' sugar, with the roasted apricots and apricot butter.

Pear & ginger waffles

The piquant ginger spice runs throughout this recipe in its many forms – ground, stem, ginger syrup and ginger wine. If you love ginger, as I do, then this is the recipe for you. Although the poached pears are delicious, if you are short of time you can substitute sliced, fresh pears instead.

260 g/2 cups self-raising/rising flour, sifted

1 teaspoon ground ginger

60 g/scant ⅓ cup caster/granulated sugar

a pinch of salt

3 eggs, separated

375 ml/1½ cups milk

2 tablespoons ginger syrup

60 g/4 tablespoons butter, melted

icing/confectioners' sugar, to dust

ginger or maple syrup, to drizzle

for the poached pears

4 ripe pears, peeled and cored, stalk intact

3 balls stem ginger preserved in syrup

80 ml/6 tablespoons ginger wine

2 tablespoons caster/granulated sugar

for the cream

2 balls stem ginger, finely chopped, plus 1 tablespoon of the preserving ginger syrup

300 ml/1¼ cups double/heavy cream

an electric or stove-top waffle iron

MAKES 8

Begin by preparing the pears. Put the pears in a saucepan or pot with the stem ginger, ginger wine and sugar and then add water to the pan until the pears are covered. Set over a medium heat and simmer for 20–30 minutes until the pears are soft. Drain the pears, discarding the liquid, and set aside to cool. Once cool, cut each pear in half, cutting through the stalk so that each pear half still has part of the stalk at the top. Thinly slice the pear but don't cut all the way through. This will mean that you can fan the pear out on top of the waffles. Set aside until you are ready to serve.

For the ginger cream, put the ginger syrup and cream in a mixing bowl and whip to soft peaks. Fold the ginger pieces into the mixture and store in the refrigerator until you are ready to serve.

To make the waffle batter, put the flour, ginger, caster/granulated sugar, salt, egg yolks, milk, ginger syrup and melted butter in a large mixing bowl. Whisk until you have a smooth batter. In a separate mixing bowl, whisk the egg whites to stiff peaks and then gently fold into the batter a third at a time.

Preheat the waffle iron and grease with a little butter.

Ladle a small amount of the batter into the preheated waffle iron and cook the waffles for 2–3 minutes until golden brown. Keep the waffles warm while you cook the remaining batter in the same way.

Serve the waffles immediately with a spoonful of the ginger cream and a poached pear half. Dust with icing/confectioners' sugar and drizzle with a little ginger syrup.

Decadent & delicious

Wake-me-up coffee pancakes

These pancakes have a real caffeine kick to wake you up. The coffee syrup is made with cocoa nibs which are a real delicacy. Cocoa nibs are fermented, dried, roasted cocoa pods, usually ground with sugar to make chocolate. They are delicious and good for you as they don't contain refined sugar but still have an amazing chocolate taste. They are available from health food stores and some supermarkets, or online.

160 g/1¼ cups self-raising/rising flour, sifted

1 teaspoon baking powder

1 egg, separated

1 tablespoon caster/granulated sugar

a pinch of salt

250 ml/1 cup iced milk coffee

3 tablespoons melted butter, plus extra for frying

150 g/1 cup mascarpone cheese

150 ml/⅔ cup crème fraîche

icing/confectioners' sugar, to taste (optional)

cocoa powder, to dust

for the syrup

100 ml/⅓ cup plus 1 tablespoon espresso coffee

60 ml/¼ cup coffee liqueur

100 g/½ cup plus 1 tablespoon caster/granulated sugar

1 teaspoon cocoa nibs or coffee beans

a large frying pan/skillet or griddle

MAKES 12

Begin by making the coffee syrup. Put all of the syrup ingredients in a saucepan or pot and simmer over a gentle heat for about 5 minutes until thick and gloopy. Set aside to allow the flavours to infuse and the syrup to cool.

To make the pancake batter, put the flour, baking powder, egg yolk, caster/granulated sugar, salt and iced coffee in a large mixing bowl and whisk together. Add in the melted butter and whisk again. The batter should have a smooth, dropping consistency.

In a separate bowl, whisk the egg white to stiff peaks. Gently fold the whisked egg white into the batter mixture using a spatula. Cover and put in the refrigerator to rest for 30 minutes.

When you are ready to serve, remove your batter mixture from the refrigerator and stir once. Put a little butter in a large frying pan/skillet set over a medium heat. Allow the butter to melt and coat the base of the pan, then ladle small amounts of the batter into the pan, leaving a little space between each. Cook until the batter is just set then turn over and cook for a further 2–3 minutes. Once cooked, keep the pancakes warm while you cook the remaining batter, adding a little butter to the pan each time, if required.

When you are ready to serve, place the mascarpone cheese and crème fraîche in a bowl, adding a little icing/confectioners' sugar to sweeten if you wish, and whisk together well.

Serve the pancakes in a stack with a dollop of the mascarpone cream on top and a drizzle of syrup. Dust with a little cocoa powder and enjoy!

Coconut chocolate pancakes

Coconut and chocolate make a great pancake combination. With a crunch of toasted, shredded coconut and coconut syrup, these pancakes are a coconut-lover's dream. If you cannot find long shredded soft coconut, substitute desiccated coconut instead.

160 g/1¼ cups self-raising/rising flour, sifted

1 teaspoon baking powder

1 egg, separated

1 teaspoon vanilla extract/vanilla bean paste

60 g/scant ⅓ cup caster/granulated sugar

a pinch of salt

250 ml/1 cup milk

3 tablespoons melted butter, plus extra for frying

100 g/⅔ cup plain/bittersweet or milk/semi-sweet chocolate chips

150 g/2 cups long shredded soft coconut

for the sauce

200 ml/¾ cup coconut milk

75 g/⅓ cup caster/granulated sugar

a large frying pan/skillet or griddle

MAKES 6

To make the pancake batter, put the flour, baking powder, egg yolk, caster/granulated sugar, salt and milk in a large mixing bowl and whisk together. Add in the melted butter and whisk again. The batter should have a smooth, dropping consistency.

In a separate bowl, whisk the egg white to stiff peaks. Gently fold the whisked egg white, the chocolate chips and half of the shredded coconut into the batter mixture using a spatula. Cover and put in the refrigerator to rest for 30 minutes.

Toast the remaining coconut in a dry frying pan until lightly golden brown. Take care to watch it closely as it can burn easily.

For the sauce, put the coconut milk and sugar in a saucepan or pot set over a medium heat and simmer for about 5 minutes until the mixture turns syrupy. Keep the pan on the heat but turn it down to low to keep the sauce warm until you are ready to serve.

When you are ready to serve, remove your batter mixture from the refrigerator and stir gently. Put a little butter in a large frying pan/skillet set over a medium heat. Allow the butter to melt and coat the base of the pan, then ladle a little of the batter into the pan. Sprinkle a tablespoon of toasted coconut over the top of the pancake and cook until the underside is golden brown and a few bubbles start to appear on the top – this will take about 2–3 minutes. Turn the pancake over using a spatula and cook on the other side until golden brown. Keep the pancakes warm while you cook the remaining batter in the same way, adding a little more butter to the pan each time if required.

Serve the pancakes warm sprinkled with the remaining toasted coconut and a drizzle of coconut sauce.

Oreo pancakes with chocolate fudge sauce

I ate these pancakes at a fantastic diner in New York and was instantly hooked. The Oreo pieces soften when cooked and create delicious chocolate bursts within the pancake. Served with a wickedly sweet chocolate sauce, these are definitely pancakes for a special treat rather than every day.

160 g/1¼ cups self-raising/rising flour, sifted

1 teaspoon baking powder

1 egg, separated

1 teaspoon vanilla extract/vanilla bean paste

2 tablespoons caster/granulated sugar

a pinch of salt

250 ml/1 cup milk

2 tablespoons melted butter, plus extra for frying

9 Oreo cookies or similar, broken into pieces

for the sauce

30 g/⅓ cup cocoa powder, sifted

1 teaspoon cold water

150 ml/⅔ cup double/heavy cream

100 g/⅓ cup milk/semi-sweet chocolate, chopped

1 tablespoon golden syrup/light corn syrup

1 tablespoon butter

a pinch of salt

1 teaspoon vanilla extract/vanilla bean paste

a large frying pan/skillet or griddle

MAKES 12

To make the pancake batter, put the flour, baking powder, egg yolk, vanilla extract/vanilla bean paste, caster/granulated sugar, salt and milk in a large mixing bowl and whisk together. Add in the melted butter and whisk again. The batter should have a smooth, dropping consistency.

In a separate bowl, whisk the egg white to stiff peaks. Gently fold the whisked egg white into the batter mixture using a spatula. Cover and put in the refrigerator to rest for 30 minutes.

For the chocolate fudge sauce, mix the cocoa powder with a little cold water until you have smooth paste. Put the cream, chocolate, cocoa paste, golden syrup/light corn syrup, butter, salt and vanilla extract in a saucepan or pot set over a medium heat and simmer until the chocolate has melted and you have a smooth, glossy sauce. Keep the pan on the heat but turn it down to low to keep the sauce warm until you are ready to serve.

When you are ready to serve, remove your batter mixture from the refrigerator and stir once. Put a little butter in a large frying pan/skillet set over a medium heat. Allow the butter to melt and coat the base of the pan, then ladle small amounts of the batter into the pan. Sprinkle some of the Oreo cookies into the batter and cook until the batter is just set then turn over and cook for a further 2–3 minutes. Once cooked, keep the pancakes warm while you cook the remaining batter in the same way, adding a little butter to the pan each time, if required.

Serve the pancakes in a stack with the hot chocolate fudge sauce poured over the top.

Mini choc chip pancakes

These mini pancakes are similar to scotch pancakes. They are plain and simple but have a hidden layer of chocolate chips in the middle. You can use any chocolate chips that you like. Although you could serve these pancakes with chocolate sauce or maple syrup – I like them just on their own with a dusting of icing sugar.

160 g/1¼ cups self-raising/rising flour, sifted

1 teaspoon baking powder

1 egg, separated

1 teaspoon vanilla extract/vanilla bean paste

2 tablespoons caster/granulated sugar

a pinch of salt

250 ml/1 cup milk

3 tablespoons melted butter, plus extra for frying

100g/⅔ cup chocolate chips (white, milk/semi-sweet, dark/ bittersweet, or a mixture of all)

icing/confectioners' sugar, for dusting

a large frying pan/skillet or griddle

MAKES 12

To make the pancake batter, put the flour, baking powder, egg yolk, caster/granulated sugar, vanilla extract/vanilla bean paste, salt and milk in a large mixing bowl and whisk together. Add in the melted butter and whisk again. The batter should have a smooth, dropping consistency.

In a separate bowl, whisk the egg white to stiff peaks. Gently fold the whisked egg white into the batter mixture using a spatula. Cover and put in the refrigerator to rest for 30 minutes.

When you are ready to serve, remove your batter mixture from the refrigerator and stir once. Put a little butter in a large frying pan/skillet set over a medium heat. Allow the butter to melt and coat the base of the pan, then ladle small amounts of batter into the pan, leaving a little space between each, and sprinkle a few chocolate chips in the centre of each pancake. Carefully spoon over a little more batter to cover the chocolate chips. Cook until the underside of each pancake is golden brown and a few bubbles start to appear on the top – this will take about 2–3 minutes. Turn the pancakes over using a spatula and cook on the other side until golden brown.

Cook the remaining batter in the same way in batches until it is all used up, adding a little butter to the pan each time, if required.

Dust with icing/confectioners' sugar and serve warm or cold.

Peanut waffles with nutty caramel ice cream

For peanut lovers, these waffles are a super treat. Bursting with peanut flavour and served with peanut butter and chocolate ice cream and a nutty caramel sauce, they are certainly not for the faint-hearted or calorie conscious! Adding honey to the sauce takes away some of the sweetness and makes it a good pouring consistency.

225 g/1¾ cups self-raising/rising flour, sifted

1 teaspoon baking powder

2 tablespoon caster/granulated sugar

3 eggs, separated

400 ml/1²⁄₃ cups milk

2 tablespoons smooth peanut butter

100 g/7 tablespoons butter, melted

for the ice cream

400 ml/1²⁄₃ cups double/heavy cream

200 ml/¾ cups milk

5 egg yolks

100 g/½ cup caster/granulated sugar

2 tablespoons peanut butter (crunchy or smooth)

for the sauce

400 ml/1²⁄₃ cups double/heavy cream

6 Snickers bars or other nut, caramel and nougat chocolate bar, chopped

2 teaspoons clear honey

an electric or stove-top waffle iron

an ice cream machine (optional, see Note)

MAKES 8

Begin by preparing the sauce. Place the cream, Snickers bars and honey in a saucepan or pot set over a medium heat and simmer until the Snickers bars have melted and the sauce is glossy. Set aside to cool.

For the ice cream, put the double/heavy cream and milk in a saucepan or pot set over a high heat and bring to the boil. In a mixing bowl, whisk together the egg yolks and caster/granulated sugar until very thick and pale yellow in colour. Pour the hot milk over the eggs in a thin stream, whisking all the time. Add the peanut butter and whisk again. Return the mixture to the pan and cook for a few minutes longer, until it begins to thicken. Leave to cool completely. Then churn in an ice cream machine following the manufacturer's instructions. Once the ice cream is almost frozen, but still soft enough to stir, stir through about a third of the chocolate peanut sauce so that it is rippled through the ice cream. Transfer to a freezer-proof container and store in the freezer until you are ready to serve.

To make the waffle batter, put the flour, baking powder, caster/ granulated sugar, salt, egg yolks, milk, peanut butter and melted butter in a large mixing bowl. Whisk until you have a smooth batter. In a separate mixing bowl, whisk the egg whites to stiff peaks and then gently fold into the batter a third at a time.

Preheat the waffle iron and grease with a little butter.

Ladle a small amount of the batter into the preheated waffle iron and cook the waffles for 2–3 minutes until golden brown. Keep the waffles warm while you cook the remaining batter in the same way.

Serve the waffles immediately with the ice cream and remaining sauce.

Note: If you do not have an ice cream machine, place the mixture in a freezer-proof container in the freezer and whisk every 20 minutes or so until frozen to break up the ice crystals. The ice cream can be stored for up to 3 months in the freezer.

S'mores waffles

Traditional s'mores use digestives biscuits/graham crackers to sandwich toasted marshmallows and chocolate together – a campsite classic! My waffle version is rich, indulgent and utterly delicious. They are definitely big enough to share – I have never known anyone to manage a whole one on their own!

260 g/2 cups self-raising/rising flour, sifted

20 g/2½ tablespoons cocoa powder, sifted

60 g/scant ⅓ cup caster/granulated sugar

a pinch of salt

3 eggs, separated

375 ml/1½ cups milk

60 g/4 tablespoons butter, melted

about 40 large marshmallows

200 g/1⅓ cup plain/bittersweet chocolate, cut into chunks, plus extra, melted, to serve

an electric or stove-top waffle iron

a chef's blow torch

MAKES 4

To make the waffle batter, put the flour, cocoa powder, caster/granulated sugar, salt, egg yolks, milk and melted butter in a large mixing bowl. Whisk until you have a smooth batter. In a separate mixing bowl, whisk the egg whites to stiff peaks and then gently fold into the batter a third at a time.

Preheat the waffle iron and grease with a little butter.

Ladle a small amount of the batter into the preheated waffle iron and cook for 2–3 minutes until crisp. Cook a second waffle in the same way.

Meanwhile cut 10 marshmallows in half and place them on top of the cooked waffle. Using the blow torch, toast the tops of the marshmallows until they are golden brown and soft. If you do not have a chef's blow torch you can toast the marshmallows under a grill. Place a quarter of the chocolate chunks on top of the toasted marshmallows, then place a second hot waffle on top and serve immediately. You need the heat of the second waffle to melt the chocolate so you need to make and serve these as you go along. Repeat with the remaining ingredients until all the batter is used up.

Serve with extra melted chocolate drizzled over the top.

Pistachio waffles

Pistachio ice cream has a delicate, perfumed flavour and is a great accompaniment to these sophisticated waffles. If you are short of time you can use store-bought pistachio or vanilla ice cream instead of making your own, but if you have time I urge you to try it as it's absolutely delicious and you'll be hooked!

100 g/¾ cup pistachios, plus a handful finely chopped, to garnish

240 g/scant 2 cups self-raising/rising flour, sifted

60 g/scant ⅓ cup caster/granulated sugar

a pinch of salt

3 eggs, separated

375 ml/1½ cups milk

60 g/4 tablespoons butter, melted

for the ice cream

100 g/¾ cup pistachios

400 ml/1⅔ cup double/heavy cream

200 ml/¾ cup milk

5 egg yolks

100 g/½ cup caster/granulated sugar

for the sauce

200 g/1⅓ cup white chocolate

250 ml/1 cup double/heavy cream

an electric or stove-top waffle iron

an ice cream machine (optional, see Note on page 54)

MAKES 8

Begin by preparing the ice cream. Put the pistachios in a food processor and pulse to a fine crumb. Transfer the finely ground pistachios to a saucepan or pot set over a high heat with the double/heavy cream and milk. Bring the mixture to the boil, then remove from the heat and leave to infuse for 30 minutes. In a mixing bowl, whisk together the egg yolks and caster/granulated sugar until very thick and pale yellow in colour. Return the pistachio milk to the heat and bring to the boil again. Pour the boiling pistachio milk over the eggs in a thin stream, whisking all the time. Return the mixture to the pan and cook for a few minutes longer until it begins to thicken. Leave to cool completely. Then churn in an ice cream machine following the manufacturer's instructions. Transfer to a freezer-proof container and store in the freezer until you are ready to serve.

For the sauce, put the white chocolate and double/heavy cream in a saucepan or pot set over a medium heat and simmer until the chocolate has melted, stirring all the time. Keep the pan on the heat but turn it down to low to keep the sauce warm until you are ready to serve.

To make the waffle batter, put the pistachios in a food processor and pulse to a fine crumb. Place the pistachios in a large mixing bowl with the flour, sugar, salt, egg yolks, milk and melted butter. Whisk until you have a smooth batter. In a separate mixing bowl, whisk the egg whites to stiff peaks and then gently fold into the batter a third at a time.

Preheat the waffle iron and grease with a little butter.

Ladle a small amount of the batter into the preheated waffle iron and cook the waffles for 2–3 minutes until golden brown. Keep the waffles warm while you cook the remaining batter in the same way.

Serve the waffles drizzled with the white chocolate sauce, topped with generous scoops of ice cream and decorated with the chopped pistachios.

Salted caramel waffles

Salted caramel gives these dessert waffles a modern twist. I could eat the sauce with anything but it is particularly delicious with hot waffles and chocolate curls. The recipe calls for vanilla salt which is available online but if you want you can make your own at home following the method given here, but be aware that it takes two weeks to create!

260 g/2 cups self-raising/rising flour, sifted

1 teaspoon baking powder

3 eggs, separated

375 ml/1½ cups milk

75 g/5 tablespoons butter, melted, plus extra for greasing

50 g/½ cup plain/bittersweet chocolate curls, to serve

for the salted caramel sauce

150 g/¾ cup caster/granulated sugar

100 g/7 tablespoons butter

1 teaspoon vanilla salt (see Note) or sea salt plus 1 teaspoon vanilla extract/vanilla bean paste

250 ml/1 cup double/heavy cream

an electric or stove-top waffle iron

MAKES 8

Begin by making the salted caramel sauce. Put the sugar and butter in a saucepan or pot set over a medium heat and simmer until both have melted and the resulting caramel starts to turn a deep golden brown. Add the salt and cream and whisk over the heat until the sauce is smooth and glossy. If any lumps of sugar have formed in your sauce, strain through a fine mesh sieve/strainer over a mixing bowl. Set aside to cool.

To make the waffle batter, put the flour, baking powder, egg yolks, milk and melted butter in a large mixing bowl. Whisk until you have a smooth batter. Add 80 ml/scant ⅓ cup of the caramel sauce and whisk again. In a separate mixing bowl, whisk the egg whites to stiff peaks and then gently fold into the batter a third at a time.

Preheat the waffle iron and grease with a little butter.

Ladle a small amount of the batter into the preheated waffle iron and cook the waffles for 3–5 minutes until golden brown. Keep the waffles warm while you cook the remaining batter in the same way.

Serve the waffles immediately with the caramel sauce on the side, topped with chocolate curls.

Note: To make vanilla salt, split 2 vanilla pods/vanilla beans and remove the seeds. Cut the pods in half. Stir the vanilla seeds into several large spoonfuls of sea salt flakes. Place the salt, seeds and vanilla pods/vanilla beans in a sterilized airtight jar and set aside for 2 weeks. Discard the vanilla pods/vanilla beans before using.

Pecan praline waffles

Making praline is not difficult and the results are so delicious. Caramelizing sugar takes a little patience but once melted the golden caramel mixes beautifully with the pecans to give a nutty crunch. It's great whipped into cream or sprinkled over these waffles.

240 g/scant 2 cups self-raising/rising flour, sifted

60 g/scant ⅓ cup caster/granulated sugar

a pinch of salt

3 eggs, separated

375 ml/1½ cups milk

100 g/½ cup pecan nuts, finely chopped

60 g/4 tablespoons butter, melted

250 ml/2 cups double/heavy cream, to serve

maple syrup, to serve

for the praline

100 g/½ cup pecan nuts

100 g/½ cup caster/granulated sugar

an electric or stove-top waffle iron

a baking sheet lined with baking parchment and greased, or a silicon mat

MAKES 8

Begin by making the praline. Heat the sugar in a dry saucepan or pot set over a medium heat until it melts and turns golden brown. Do not stir the sugar but swirl it from time to time to prevent it from burning. Scatter the pecans onto the prepared baking sheet then pour the sugar caramel over the nuts and leave to set. Once cool, transfer the praline sheet to a food processor and pulse to a fine crumb. Store in an airtight container until you are ready to serve. The praline is best made on the day you are using it as it can become sticky when exposed to the air.

To make the waffle batter, put the flour, caster/granulated sugar, salt, egg yolks, milk, chopped pecans and melted butter in a large mixing bowl. Whisk until you have a smooth batter. In a separate mixing bowl, whisk the egg whites to stiff peaks and then gently fold into the batter a third at a time.

Preheat the waffle iron and grease with a little butter.

Ladle a small amount of the batter into the preheated waffle iron and cook the waffles for 2–3 minutes until golden brown. Keep the waffles warm while you cook the remaining batter in the same way.

Put the cream in a bowl with half of the praline and whisk to stiff peaks.

Serve the waffles with a spoonful of praline cream, drizzled with maple syrup and sprinkled with the remaining pecan praline.